KAVITHA MANDANA has written books for children published by Talking Cub, Puffin (Penguin), Karadi Tales, Pratham, Red Turtle (Rupa). Her short fiction has appeared in various anthologies as well as in school English textbooks. She's been writing and illustrating for the *Deccan Herald*'s children's supplement for the past twenty years.

The Story of India's National EMBLEM

Kavitha Mandana

Illustrations by Dhwani Ved

talking CUB
An Imprint of Speaking Tiger Books

TALKING CUB

Published by Speaking Tiger Books LLP
125A, Ground Floor, Shahpur Jat,
Near Asiad Village, New Delhi 110 049

First published in paperback in Talking Cub
by Speaking Tiger Books in 2024

ISBN: 978-93-5447-883-3

eISBN: 978-93-5447-768-3

10 9 8 7 6 5 4 3 2 1

Book design by Dhwani Ved
Typeset in Cardo by Jojy Philip
Printed at Chaman Enterprises, New Delhi

'CAN WE HAVE SOME NEW ENVELOPES, PLEASE?'

It was the morning of 22 July 1947.

Members of India's newly elected Constituent Assembly were getting ready for one of their many lively debates. There were 299 of them, and they were drafting independent India's very own, brand new Constitution.

The members of this Assembly had gathered in a building that was, at the time, called Council House. (Council House became our Parliament building post-Independence, and was the seat of the Legislature, till 2023.) It had been built and inaugurated just twenty years earlier by the British after they moved their capital from Calcutta (now Kolkata) to New Delhi. The imposing new buildings laid out across Raisina Hill by architects Edward Lutyens and Herbert Baker were designed to project imperial power, to reflect the might of the British.

Ensemble of Government buildings on Kartavyapath (earlier Rajpath) in New Delhi

When these monumental structures were planned for the new capital city of New Delhi, the cost was initially estimated to be 4-5 million pounds. Due to the delays caused by World War II, eventually the cost was 10 million pounds! In today's value, this would be approximately 819 million pounds, or almost 91 billion rupees. Evidently, the British believed it was a worthwhile investment since they thought they would govern India forever from these buildings!

But just twenty tumultuous years after the inauguration, the people seated at the grand circular Council House were not British colonial rulers, but 299 Indians. In this building designed by the Englishman Herbert Baker, Indians began the process of governing themselves.

That July morning, as the session began, Assembly member Ram Narayan Singh from Bihar stood up to speak. Addressing Dr Rajendra Prasad, the President of the Constituent Assembly, he said:

‘Sir, I wish to draw your attention to a very important constitutional issue. I think, and everybody knows, that we are meeting as a sovereign body here and making the Constitution for a Free India. But in the envelopes used by the Assembly Office we still find on the top, the words “On His Majesty’s Service”. I think this is not proper and I draw the attention of the House and yourself to this matter. I hope these words will be dropped from the envelopes in future in the correspondence conducted by the Assembly Office.’

Ram Narayan Singh

It was time for India to replace the words ‘On His Majesty’s Service’ not only on official envelopes and letterheads, but also from currency notes, postage stamps, and official government documents. India needed to have her very own National Emblem!

The same day, Jawaharlal Nehru rose to pass a resolution regarding the Indian flag. Nehru's speech was an emotional one—full of hope about India's future. In this speech, what Nehru said about using the Ashoka Chakra (or Dharma Chakra) on the national flag, is equally applicable to what eventually became India's National Emblem—the four lions that once sat atop a 50-foot Ashoka pillar.

Now because I have mentioned the name of Ashoka, I should like you to think that the Ashokan period in Indian history was essentially an international period of Indian history. It was not a narrowly national period. It was a period when India's ambassadors went abroad to far countries not in the way of an Empire and imperialism but as ambassadors of peace and culture and goodwill.'

Ashoka pillar at Vaishali, Bihar

In response to these lines, the packed hall broke into applause. The words resonated with the audience, a majority of whom were freedom fighters. These men and women were brave survivors of countless lathi charges, indiscriminate police firings, jail terms, and endless harassment by the British administration in India.

In June 1947, Lord Mountbatten had announced that the British would leave India, and the country would be divided into two nations—India and Pakistan—and this came to be known as the Partition of India. The initial schedule had the handover of rule to Indians on 8 June 1948. This would have given the British, Indian, and the newly-formed state of Pakistan adequate time to plan for the new reality. (To add to the complexity of the handover, Pakistan itself was to be a bifurcated country, with one part separated from the other by thousands of kilometres into West and East Pakistan.)

However, this plan changed, and the British decided to leave earlier, in August 1947. This meant that the Indians had to accelerate their preparations for self-governance. The Constituent Assembly set up to draft the new Constitution would take close to three years to complete their task. But this was too long a period for a proud new country to continue using old symbols of the British Raj.

Free India needed a National Emblem that represented its new status amongst the free nations of the world. The emblem also needed to represent its constitutional philosophy.

By the end of the session on 22 July 1947, the matter of India's flag got settled. With 15 August, India's first Independence Day barely three weeks away, a flag to replace the Union Jack was an urgent matter.

Deciding on the National Emblem would take a few more months. It was only in December 1947 that the capital of the Ashoka pillar at Sarnath, with the words 'Satyameva Jayate' written below it in Devanagiri, got adopted as our National Emblem.

In the 1800s, nineteen Ashoka pillars had been rediscovered across northern India and the Brahmi inscriptions on them had been deciphered. Of these pillars, only six had their carved capitals (the top of the pillar) relatively intact. The four lions of the Sarnath capital were chosen for what they represented—power, courage, confidence and pride.

DR AMBEDKAR

Among the 299 members of India's Constituent Assembly, there was no one else with as many internationally recognized qualifications as Bhimrao Ambedkar. He had two doctorates in Economics—one from Columbia University, New York and the other from the University of London. When he moved to Britain after his studies in the US, he began studying Law even while he enrolled at the London School of Economics to write another thesis.

It is no wonder that Indian Nobel Laureate and economist Amartya Sen stated that Ambedkar was the highest educated Indian economist of ALL time!

Naturally, he was among the seven members selected to draft the Constitution and chair the Drafting Committee. After Independence, he was free India's first Law Minister.

'TRUTH ALONE TRIUMPHS'

With the National Emblem, the Constituent Assembly was digging deep into India's rich past for inspiration.

India's freedom fighters were sure of the path they did NOT want to take for the newly independent nation—that of the British model of conquest and endless wars. India had been forced to fight in two World Wars for the British rulers. Over a million Indians fought in World War I, which was supposed to bring about 'lasting peace'. But the 60,000 Indians who died in distant lands, fighting for a British victory, gave up their lives for a lost cause. Instead of peace, merely twenty years later, World War II broke out.

This time, around 3 million Indians went into the battlefields across the globe to fight on the side of the British.

Over 75,000 Indians died fighting in World War II, and over 3 million more died in the Bengal Famine of 1943 that occurred due to food supply shortages because of the war. The British administrators sent food grains from India to their armies across the globe instead of feeding the starving Indians.

To those drafting the Constitution for a free India, the rewards of war seemed to be yet more wars—the two World Wars had proved that. On the other hand, the rewards of non-violence seemed far higher. It was through a primarily non-violent freedom struggle that India had defeated the far more wealthy, powerful, and well-armed British.

Indian soldiers at a shore post in Berbera, Somalia, August 1940

Gandhiji's Salt March, the Satyagraha Movement, the Civil Disobedience Movement, had all turned India from 'the Jewel in the British Crown' to an extremely difficult and non-profitable place to govern.

Gandhiji leading the famous 1930 Salt March

In looking to the past, India's freedom fighters settled on Emperor Ashoka, the third ruler of the Mauryan dynasty. He had ruled between 268 BCE – 232 BCE. Ashoka's life story resonated with the leaders of a new India. He had come to power by overthrowing his elder step-brother whom his father Bindusara had anointed Crown Prince. Through continuous war he had expanded the Mauryan Empire into one of the largest in the world. Yet, after his victory in the brutal Kalinga battle, he was struck by remorse at the scale of destruction and formally renounced war. He converted to Buddhism and for the rest of his reign, preached non-violence.

Emperor Ashoka

DECODING WHAT THOSE FOUR LIONS ARE TRYING TO TELL US

On the Indian currency note, we see the capital atop the Ashoka pillar with three lions seated with their backs to each other. They are sitting on a drum, or abacus, as it is called in architectural terms. Below the feet of the central lion is the Ashoka Chakra or Dharma Chakra. It is a wheel with twenty-four spokes flanked by a horse and a bull on either side.

When we look at a photograph of the lion capital at Sarnath, we

What the Ashoka pillar in Sarnath would have looked like with the large chakra above the lions intact

realize that the beautifully carved sandstone sculpture actually has four lions. And on the abacus there are four Dharma Chakras with twenty-four spokes in each one. The chakras are interspersed by four animals and they seem to be moving in a clockwise direction. The animals are the bull, horse, elephant, and the lion.

The capital is about 7 feet tall and has been carved from a single slab of sandstone. In the image chosen for the National Emblem, the inverted lotus below the abacus has been replaced by the words 'Satyameva Jayate'

Lion Capital at Sarnath

WHY LIONS?

The Buddha

Ashoka had embraced Buddhism in a very dramatic manner. After a big victory in the battle against Kalinga, he was struck by deep remorse, horrified by the suffering caused by his own actions. The life and the words of the Buddha guided him out of that dark phase. It was after this that he set up edicts on pillars and rock faces all across his kingdom. In these, he spoke directly to the people about how the emperor had given up warfare; or told them his plans to make life more comfortable for the citizens of his vast kingdom. While most of the Ashokan edicts have less to do with Buddhism and are more to do with him, they did use a number of Buddhist symbols.

The Buddha himself was from the Shakya clan of chieftains. He was referred to as Shakyasimha (the Lion of the Shakyas). Ashoka would have also found these animals attractive since they are a symbol of royalty.

Of the seven pillars discovered in various stages of ruin, only the one at Vaishali (where Buddha preached his last sermon) is in pristine condition. Its single-lion capital is intact, and is still perched on top of the tall sandstone shaft. All the other pillars have been discovered in broken condition, the capital buried nearby along with other debris. Lions, either single or in fours, have been found on most of the capitals. The exceptions are the capital found in Rampurva (near Champaran in Bihar), with a bull carved on it. This is displayed in the old Parliament building. Another one is the elephant capital that was found at Sunkissa, an ancient Buddhist site near Kanauj (UP).

THE CHAKRA

This is loaded with symbolism. For Buddhists, it is the Wheel of Law or the Dharma Wheel that Buddha set in motion when he preached his first sermon at Sarnath.

For kings, the wheel has other connotations. For instance, the term Chakravartin implies a ruler of vast territories through whose good governance, the Wheel of Dharma (Wheel of Law) keeps turning.

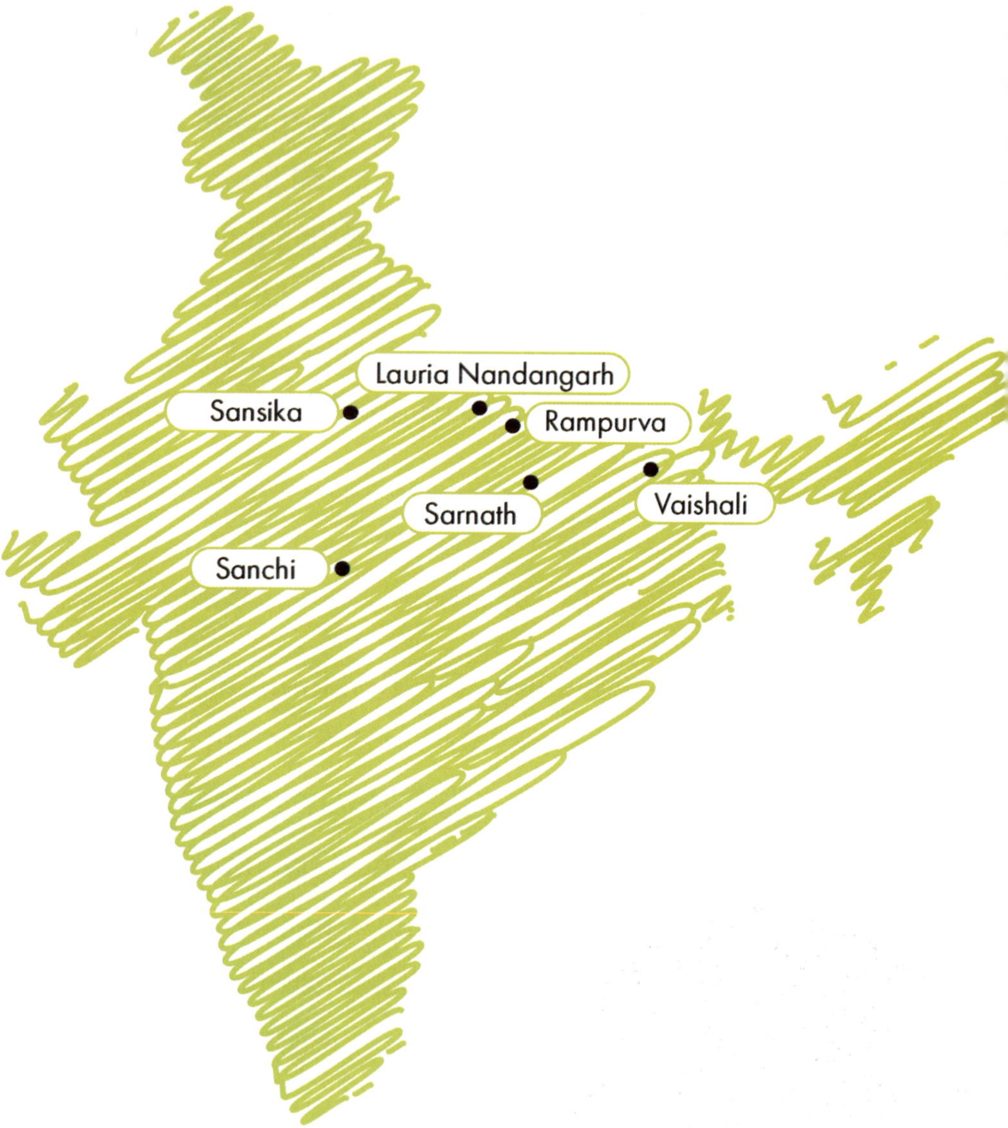

Locations of Ashoka pillars

THE FOUR ANIMALS

Scholars suggest that the animals walking on the abacus below the lions are linked to four key events in the Buddha's life. The bull stands for Buddha's astrological sign Vrishabha (Taurus). The horse is Kantaka, the one the Buddha, as Siddhartha, rode to escape his father's palace, marking a break from his life of luxury. In all print and 2D representations of the national emblem, only the horse and bull are visible.

The lion represents his lineage from the Shakyas. And the elephant represents the dream his mother, Queen Maya had, of a white elephant with six tusks entering her womb from her side.

ASHOKA AND BUDDHISM

Ashoka adopted Buddhism, but members of his family followed different religions. His father, Bindusara, was an Ajvika (a sect somewhat like atheists), his mother Subhadrangi was a Brahmin, and his grandfather, Chandragupta Maurya, was a Jain.

The Mauryan court had close relations with the Greek kingdoms in the north-west that had grown with the arrival of Alexander's army on the banks of the Indus river, just a generation earlier. There were immense cultural exchanges with the Iranian Archaeminid kingdom bordering the Mauryan lands to the west. In fact, art historians claim that the pillars of Ashoka, as well as the style of the lions show influences from the Archaeminid neighbours of that era.

So while the symbolism of the lion capital is strongly linked to Buddhism, the edicts etched on the pillars and on rock faces across India were mostly secular. The edicts advertised Ashoka's good deeds, among other things, like the trees planted along highways to make life easier for travellers. The edicts on rocks and pillars close to the empire's borders reassured neighbouring countries that Ashoka did not aim to conquer their territories. Some edicts even have details on taxation.

The few pillars that had edicts linked to Ashoka's own religion were at Buddhist pilgrimage sites like Sanchi (where Ashoka built the famous stupa under which the Buddha's relics were buried). Those were stern lectures directed at Buddhists telling them not to create divisions within Buddhism.

WHAT GOT LEFT OUT FROM OUR EMBLEM

When the Sarnath pillar and capital were discovered, the pillar was broken in many places. The capital was discovered a few metres away, buried under centuries of rubble. At first glance, it appeared that the capital was entirely undamaged—a truly rare case. But later, broken parts of a much larger thirty-two-spoked chakra were found. This would have been fixed on top of the shoulders of the four lions. A picture of the original Ashoka capital displayed at the Archaeological Survey of India's on-site museum in Sarnath shows where the bigger chakra would have been positioned.

The bell-shaped inverted lotus on which the abacus sits was also dropped from the National Emblem.

WHICH OTHER COUNTRY HAS THE DHARMA CHAKRA IN ITS NATIONAL EMBLEM?

If you answered 'Sri Lanka', you're correct!

While Buddhism had died out across India by the 12th century CE, it was widely practiced in Sri Lanka from Ashokan times to the present day. Just as Hindus make up the majority of India's population, Buddhists are the majority in Sri Lanka.

Ashoka's son Mahendra, and daughter Sanghamitra, visited Sri Lanka to spread the message of the Buddha and the local royal families adopted the new religion. The Sri Lankan text *Mahavamsa* records the arrival of the Mauryan siblings on the island.

The words that appear below the lions on the National Emblem are: 'Satyameva Jayate'. It is a Sanskrit phrase, which means 'Truth alone triumphs'. It is from the Mundaka Upanishad, which was composed nearly 3,000 years ago!

The Mundaka Upanishad is in the Atharva Veda, composed approximately between 1200 BCE and 900 BCE. It is one of the five Mukhya Upanishads among the 108 that are known to us today. It is also the shortest one and the most translated.

Among other topics, the Mundaka Upanishad offers guidance on leading a good life, the concepts around the auspicious word 'Om', advice on medical practices, herbal remedies, and a lot more. Like the Bhagavat Gita, which is presented as a conversation between Lord Krishna and Arjuna before the battle at Kurukshetra in the Mahabharata, the Mundaka Upanishad is also a conversation (in verse). A pious householder Saunaka asks Sage Angiras, 'Sir, what is that through which, if it is known, everything else becomes known?'

And over a series of verses, the learned sage replies. To paraphrase his words, he tells Saunaka that according to sages who have attained one-ness with Brahman (the

Universe), there are two kinds of knowledge—the lower one involves learning the Vedas, rituals, scriptures and other religious practices. But the release from continuous rebirth (samsara) only comes from true knowledge of oneself, attained through deep meditation, yoga, etc. 'Satyameva Jayate' appears in the first khanda of the third Mundaka.

Here is the verse this motto has been taken from:

सत्यमेव जयते नानृतं सत्येन पन्था विततो देवयानः।
येनाक्रमन्त्यृषयो ह्याप्तकामा यत्र तत् सत्यस्य परमं निधानम्॥

Satyameva jayate nanṛataṃ satye na pantha vitato devayanaḥ |
Yenakramantyṛṣayo hyaptakama yatra tat satyasya paramam nidhanam ||

Translation:
Truth alone triumphs; not falsehood.
Through truth the divine path is spread out
by which the sages whose desires have been completely fulfilled,
reach that supreme treasure of Truth.

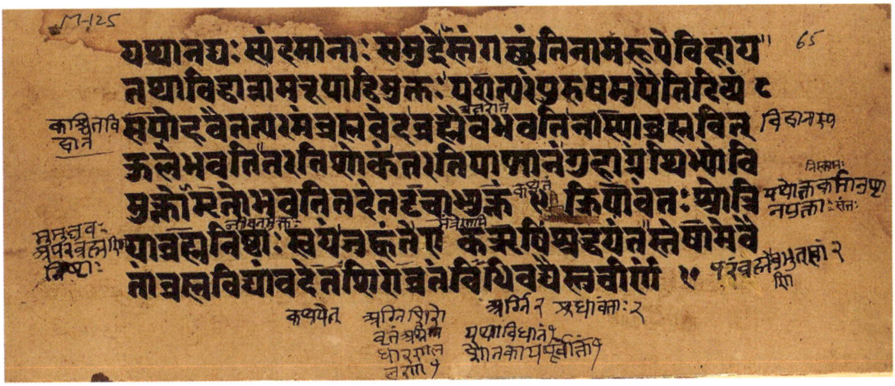

DATING TEXTS THAT HAVE NO DATE ON THEM

You might wonder how is it possible to fix the date of a text that is thousands of years old and for which we have no original copy. In such cases, what the text mentions gives historians their clues. In the case of the Atharva Veda (the last of the four Vedas to be written), it is here that iron ore is mentioned for the first time in Indian texts. So the text can be dated to India's early Iron Age (1200 BCE to 900 BCE).

WHERE THE FOUR LIONS BEGAN THEIR JOURNEY

Ashoka's pillars, erected across multiple locations along the River Ganga, on an average weighed about 50 tons and ranged in height from 30 to 50 feet. So how did such heavy slabs of sandstone get transported from Chunar, a quarry close to Mirzapur in UP, to places like Sarnath, Sanchi, Bodh Gaya, Lauria Nandangarh and other locations where Ashoka had pillars installed?

The Chunar stone quarry is still active! But now, flat slabs called pathia, of about 3–4 feet, that are used for roofing are prepared here, and not mammoth pillars ordered by an emperor. These smaller slabs are simply loaded onto trucks and taken away.

In the Mauryan era, transporting heavy 50-ton slabs required ingenuity. You will notice that all Ashoka's pillars are circular. That had less to do with the architect's design, and more to simplify the first stage of transport.

Archaeologist Professor Vidula Jayaswal, whose extensive field work at Chunar began in 1990, has a lot of interesting details to report. First, slabs of the required thickness were quarried at Chunar. Then its sharp edges were chiselled away, on site, so that the pillars became cylindrical in shape. This made it very simple to roll these heavy pillar shafts downhill to the river bank. From there, they were loaded onto barges and transported to river ports closest to the spots where they would be installed.

Professor Jayaswal spent three years studying 10 square km of this region.

She found over 450 quarries back in the 1990s. More have been discovered since. At the bottom of the hillside where the quarries are, the professor recorded 1,128 cylindrical blocks of varying lengths, and even blocks with inscriptions that have been read and translated by renowned epigraphists.

One wonders why these stones didn't get shipped out. Did some 'quality inspector' arrive and decide they weren't of the right thickness or length? Or would the emperor's death in 232 BCE mean all work on pillar installation stopped entirely?

These inscriptions at Chunar are not the grand words dictated by an emperor but contain practical details chiselled by artisans. For instance, the name of the artisans, which probably indicated who the slabs had to be delivered to at the installation site. Apart from chiselling away the sharp edges and turning them into cylinders, all other work like the carving of the capitals and the polishing of the pillar, happened later at the installation sites like Sanchi, Sarnath, etc.

The Chunar inscriptions date from the same Mauryan period, with the artisans' names written in Kharoshti (suggesting that these craftsmen might have migrated from the north-western part of the Mauryan empire, or from the bordering Archaeminid empire.

RIGHT-TO-LEFT....LEFT-TO-RIGHT

The two main scripts used on Ashoka's pillars and rock edicts were Brahmi and Kharoshti. In the eastern and southern parts of the empire, Brahmi was used to write edicts in the Prakrit language, just as the Devanagiri script is used to write innumerable modern languages like Hindi, Marathi, as well as an ancient language like Sanskrit.

In the extreme western and north-western parts of the Mauryan empire, the Kharoshti script was used to write languages like Prakrit, as well as Greek and Aramaic.

In fact, Kharoshti could be written bi-directionally and is read from left to right on the first line and right to left on the second, pretty much how you move from 1-100 on a Snakes and Ladder board game. This style is called boustrophedon and early Greek was written in this manner.

TWO PILLARS EMBARK ON A SECOND BOAT RIDE

Feroz Shah Tughluq

By the 1300s, Buddhism had virtually died out across India. The last prominent dynasties to patronize the religion were the Palas and Senas in the Bengal and Bihar region. Besides, no one understood the Brahmi and Kharoshti scripts any longer. And neither was the Prakrit language being spoken.

When Feroz Shah Tughluq, who ruled from Delhi in the fourteenth century CE, went hunting and campaigning across his kingdom in the 1350s, he came across two of Ashoka's pillars—one at Topra, near Ambala, and the other near Meerut.

Since no one could read the script, it wasn't possible to decipher the edicts etched on the pillars. Yet, Feroz Shah still found them impressive and wanted to transport them back to his new capital near Delhi—Ferozabad. He planned on erecting one pillar at his palace in Ferozabad and the other close to his hunting lodge.

Feroz Shah's engineers fabricated elaborate forty-two-wheeled carts to transport the tall pillars to the banks of River Yamuna from where they were loaded onto barges that sailed to Delhi.

Both are still upright and can be seen today, though without their capitals. It is unclear if the capitals still capped the pillars in the 1350s when Feroz Shah found the standing pillars, or whether they were damaged later.

The Ashoka pillar at Ferozabad

HOW ASHOKA'S LIONS WERE RE-DISCOVERED

Weighing on average about 50 tons and towering up to heights of 30–40 feet, Ashoka had these pillars installed so that he could speak directly to not just the common people across his empire but also those across borders AND across generations.

Yet, these seemingly indestructible structures played hide and seek with history. When Chinese Buddhist scholars visited India on pilgrimage and to study Buddhist texts, they reported seeing these massive

Faxian

Hiuen Tsang

pillars at pilgrim centres like Buddha's birthplace in Lumbini. The Chinese monk Seng-Tsai was the earliest to record his Buddhist pilgrimage. Later, a sixty-year-old monk, Faxian (who spent ten years in India) mentioned visiting Lumbini and other sites. And by the time Hiuen Tsang came in the seventh century CE, many Buddhist pilgrim sites and pillars were in a state of neglect. With Buddhism losing popularity, many sites got abandoned altogether.

After appearing in the travelogues of these Chinese Buddhist visitors, Ashoka's pillars made another brief appearance in the historical record when Feroz Shah discovered two of them and shipped them to Delhi. A few centuries later, when the British arrived in India, many Buddhist sites began to be excavated.

In 1815, Colin MacKenzie, the first director of the newly established Archaeological Survey of India (ASI) began excavating at Sarnath, the spot where Buddha gave his first sermon in 528 BCE. Alexander Cunningham, another ASI director, then worked on the site between 1833 – 1836.

Colin MacKenzie

Alexander Cunningham

Friedrich Oscar Oertel

Yet, it took a German, Friedrich Oscar Oertel, working in British India as a PWD engineer, to discover the pillar and capital that the two ASI directors had missed! In 1903, while posted at Benares, he got a permit to excavate at Sarnath. That's when Ashoka's pillar (broken into three parts) was discovered, and close to the Dhameka stupa, Oertel's team dug up the pillar's capital—the same one that is now our National Emblem. During the course of this dig, his team discovered many other treasures—a statue of a Bodhisattva, the foundations of a monastery, forty-one inscriptions, and over 400 sculptural remains.

Oertel wasn't necessarily a better archaeologist than the two ASI directors. He just had seventy more years of additional research to guide him. When MacKenzie and Cunningham were digging at Sarnath, the translations of the edicts of Ashoka had not all been published yet. Historians had still not identified Ashoka as the emperor who is named as 'Devanampriya' on the inscriptions.

When Oertel set out to excavate at Sarnath in 1903, he knew what he was looking for, because a few of Ashoka's pillars had already been discovered and their edicts translated. Sadly, he didn't get a chance to come back for another season of excavation as there was a famine the following year and then he got transferred out of the region.

THE NATIONAL EMBLEM AND A YOUNG ARTIST FROM HYDERABAD

Badruddin Tyabji

In the search for the National Emblem, Jawaharlal Nehru turned to an Indian Civil Service officer whose family had played a key role in the freedom struggle for three generations. Badruddin Tyabji was named after his illustrious grandfather who became the first Indian solicitor (with British qualifications) to practice in India, and eventually became the first Indian Chief Justice of the Bombay High Court. He was also a key member of the

Indian National Congress. After Independence, Badruddin Tyabji served as India's first ambassador to Belgium, before moving to many other places across the world.

By choosing Badruddin to head the search for a national emblem, Nehru was also inadvertently tapping into the talents of Badruddin's wife, Surayya Tyabji (earlier Hydari), who was a well-known artist. Surayya belonged to the Hydari family from present-day Telangana, which boasted of a long list of high-ranking bureaucrats, freedom fighters AND three generations of educated women.

An all-India competition was announced, and art students from across the country were invited to design the new National Emblem. Sadly, most of the designs proved to be derivative—taking inspiration from the British lion-and-unicorn coat-of-arms.

Surayya Tyabji was already a member of the Flag Presentation Committee in the Constituent Assembly. She and her husband felt that the Ashoka capital would make an excellent National Emblem. As an artist, the twenty-eight-year-old Surayya had a great appreciation for Mauryan art and sculpture. So she drew the lions, and managed to get the printing press of the Viceregal Lodge to make copies that could be distributed to members of the Constituent Assembly, so they could judge.

Surayya Tyabji

The rest is history. The design for the National Emblem was quickly approved, and it has been the symbol of the Republic of India ever since.

THE MANUSCRIPT OF INDIA'S CONSTITUTION: A UNIQUE WORK OF ART

The long process of drafting the Constitution began on 22 January 1947, when Nehru moved the Objectives Resolution at the Constituent Assembly and it was adopted. From then on, the momentum for Indian Independence picked up pace.

On 29 August 1947, just weeks after Independence, the Constituent Assembly set up the Drafting Committee, and the very next day, Dr B.R. Ambedkar was voted as its Chairman. As this important task of writing down the legal framework for a free India went on, everyone involved was acutely aware of what a momentous event India's Independence was, in the history of the world.

The most powerful empire on earth had been driven out of India. Countless countries across Asia and Africa that were still colonised by the British or other European powers, were looking to India for inspiration.

THE CALLIGRAPHISTS

At this time, Jawaharlal Nehru reached out to a number of renowned artists. He wanted India's Constitution to not just be a powerful legal document but also a work of art.

One of the artists who was approached was Prem Behari Narain Raizada, a renowned calligraphist. Nehru asked him if he would be interested in being the calligraphist for the Constitution. He planned on having two copies of the Constitution (one in English and the other in Hindi) hand-lettered and hand-illustrated on parchment paper. These hand-made books would continue the long tradition of India's palm leaf manuscripts and illuminated Mughal books.

Raizada agreed to take on this prestigious assignment and even refused to charge for his work. His only condition was to be able to sign his name on each hand-lettered page and include his grandfather's name on the last page.

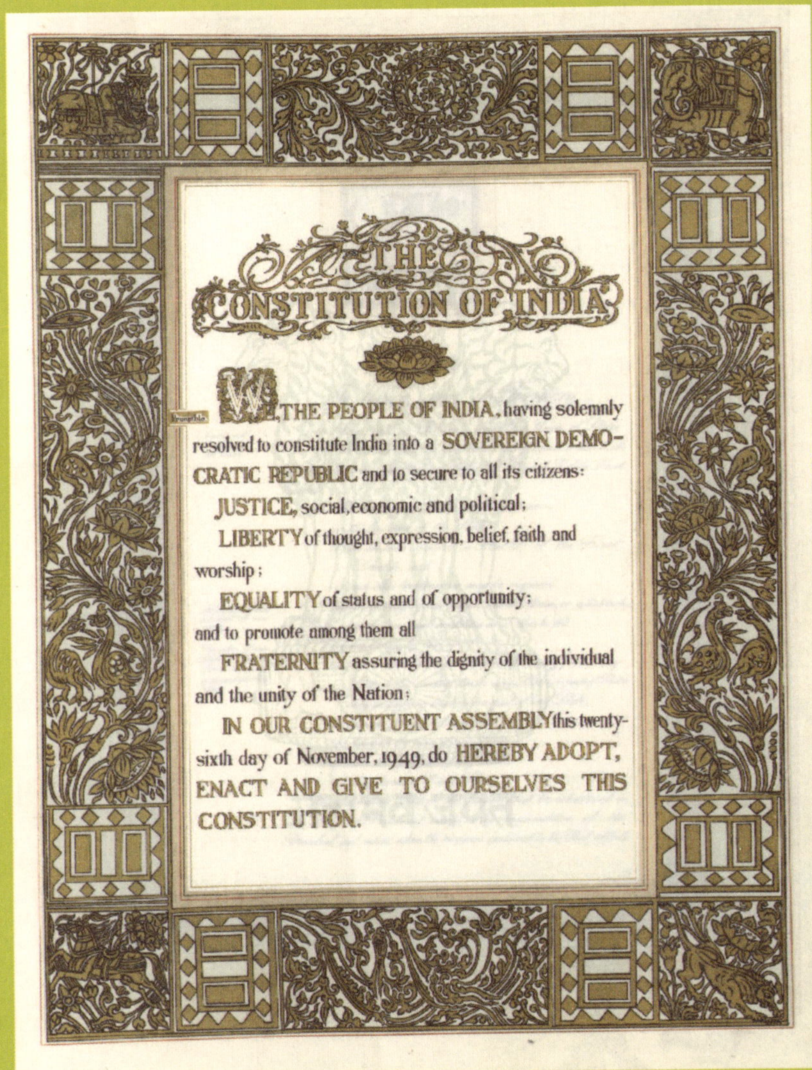

THE

CONSTITUTION OF INDIA

WE, THE PEOPLE OF INDIA, having solemnly resolved to constitute India into a SOVEREIGN DEMOCRATIC REPUBLIC and to secure to all its citizens:

JUSTICE, social, economic and political;

LIBERTY of thought, expression, belief, faith and worship;

EQUALITY of status and of opportunity;

and to promote among them all

FRATERNITY assuring the dignity of the individual and the unity of the Nation;

IN OUR CONSTITUENT ASSEMBLY this twenty-sixth day of November, 1949, do HEREBY ADOPT, ENACT AND GIVE TO OURSELVES THIS CONSTITUTION.

Preamble of the Constitution of India

Raizada came from a family of well-known calligraphists. He had lost his parents early and was brought up by his grandfather, Ram Prashadji Saxena, who taught his grandson the craft. Nehru was happy to agree to the terms.

As Raizada began hand-writing the Constitution at Constitution Hall (now the Constitution Club), he was joined by Vasant Krishan Vaidya, the calligraphist selected to write the Constitution in Hindi.

As the two artists laboured away at their task, other artists got to work.

NANDALAL BOSE AND THE KALA BHAVAN STUDENTS FROM SHANTINIKETAN

Nandalal Bose

Nandalal Bose, the principal of the art college at Shantiniketan was asked to illustrate the Constitution. This turned into a dream assignment for a number of young art college students. There was a lot of work to be completed—each of the 251 large (16x22 inch) pages of the Constitution needed a hand-illustrated border. The title pages of each of the twenty-two parts of the document needed a painting. And some pages needed elaborate gold-leaf borders and lettering.

A team of twenty-two students got to work. Luckily, we have the names of some of them—Beohar Rammanohar Sinha, for instance. He is the artist who painted the Harappan seal on Page 1 of the Constitution, Vikramaditya and his coin/seal on Page 104, the Nalanda seal on Page 105, the Nataraja on Page 113, Subhas Chandra Bose on Page 160, and many others. Rather remarkably, Rammanohar refused to sign his name on the paintings that he did.

Dinanath Bhargava is another artist we know about. He is famous for illustrating the National Emblem. Even prior to Nehru's invitation to artists, Dinanath had been interested in painting lions and had spent many hours observing and sketching them at the Kolkata zoo. So, once the Ashoka pillar capital was selected as our National Emblem, Nandalal Bose picked this young artist to illustrate it. He not only had to render it in line-drawing for letterheads and other media, but he also painted it for the first page of the Constitution.

Eventually, when the two beautifully bound, hand-written and illustrated copies of the Constitution were ready, 1,000 lithographic prints were made from these originals to be placed in important libraries. And to preserve the original manuscripts for posterity, they are stored in a hermetically sealed, helium-filled case and displayed at the Parliament Museum.

The National Emblem illustrated

by Dinanath Bhargava

NANDALAL BOSE (1882 – 1966) AND THE FREEDOM STRUGGLE

Nandalal Bose's artistic evolution ran parallel to India's freedom struggle. In Kolkata, while he studied art under Abanindranath Tagore, he also came into contact with various other artists, folk art traditions and the Chinese and Japanese styles of painting. From Sister Nivedita, he absorbed more avant garde ideas on the role of art in building a nation.

Gandhiji's sensationally successful Dandi March and the Salt Satyagraha inspired him tremendously. His iconic sketches, prints and paintings made from photographs of Gandhiji marching, grabbed the nation's attention.

In 1938, the Congress party was holding its 51st session in the village of Haripura in Gujarat. For this, Gandhiji personally commissioned Bose to paint panels for the event. The Mahatma's brief to Bose was to remember that most of his viewers will be rural folk, so the art ought to appeal to them.

After touring the surrounding regions extensively, Bose painted 400 posters for the event. These are now famously known as the Haripura murals and are studied by art students even today.

With such deep connections to the freedom movement, it was but natural that he would be approached to oversee the important task of illustrating the new country's brand new Constitution!

Gandhiji Praying by Nandalal Bose

LION SPOTTING

What are the chances that the four lions from the National Emblem reside within your home? If anyone in your family is a Member of Parliament, they are authorized to use the National Emblem on their letterheads for official communication. In that case, there would be very elegant stationery lying around—but NOT for you to use for your letter writing! Know someone in the Indian Police Service? Then the four lions can be seen in the uniform and on their peaked caps.

If you have an Aadhar card, you have your very own National Emblem right there! All currency notes have the Ashoka lion capital on them. Indian passports have the

National Emblem embossed on them. And when you turn eighteen and get your first driver's licence, you will be carrying around this beautiful symbol of our Constitution in your wallet every time you drive a car.

But unlike our National Flag that we can wave and display with patriotic fervor on Independence Day or Republic Day, or whenever our sports team is playing another country, there are very strict rules about who can use the National Emblem and where it can be used.

A list of locations where the National Emblem can be spotted within India:

1. Parliament House
2. State Legislature buildings like the Vidhana Soudha in Bengaluru (Karnataka), the Vidhan Sabha in Mumbai, etc
3. Rashtrapati Bhawan
4. All the Raj Bhawans (where the Governors stay)
5. The Supreme Court
6. All High Courts
7. Central Secretariat Buildings
8. Secretariat Buildings of the State Governments or UT Governments.

Homesick Indians abroad can find our beloved National Emblem in the following places:

1. At the Indian Consulates/Embassies
2. On the premises of the heads of missions (like ambassadors) representing India in other countries

HOW TO AVOID A 2-YEAR PRISON TERM AND/OR A RS 2000 FINE!

There are many laws that spell out clearly exactly how our National Emblem can be used. According to some of them:

1. Individuals or organizations can NOT use the National Emblem.
2. The Emblems & Names (Prevention of Improper Use) Act, 1950, and the Emblems & Names (Prevention of Improper Use) Rules, 1982, also restrict which particular governmental agencies are authorized to use the National Emblem on buildings, uniforms or stationery.
3. Section 4 of the State Emblem of India (Prohibition of Improper Use) Act, 2005, states that no individual or organization may use the National Emblem for company registration, patent registration, or any other purpose unless the Central Government grants permission.
4. Section 5 of this Act also bans registration authorities from registering any business, trade, or patent that includes the emblem in their logo or official symbols.

Not following these rules can land a person in prison, or having to pay a hefty fine.

The National Emblem is supposed to inspire a sense of deep loyalty and pride among the citizens of a country. And our majestic four lions certainly inspire those emotions in us.

Great kings renouncing their way of life is rare. The Buddha, a Shakya prince, did it before Ashoka. Ashoka's grandfather, Chandragupta Maurya, renounced his throne when a famine swept through his kingdom. But the most inspiring example is that of Ashoka who changed his path after a resounding victory in battle!

Similarly, as Indians who enjoy our freedom in the twenty-first century, we forget that back in the 1930s, nobody in the world (least of all the English) ever dreamt that the back of the great British Empire would be broken by non-violent protests in India.

So really, the power the four lions represent is NOT brute strength, but the strength that comes when justice and truth is on one's side—as it was when India's freedom fighters took on the military might of the British Raj...and won!

PHOTO CREDITS

Page 5, Jawaharlal Nehru and other members taking pledge during the midnight session of the Constituent Assembly of India held on 14 and 15 August 1947, Wikimedia Commons

Page 6-7, Ensemble of Government buildings on Kartavyapath (earlier Rajpath) in New Delhi, Wikimedia Commons

Page 8, Parliament House, Wikimedia Commons

Page 10, British official envelope, Wikimedia Commons

Page 11, Ashokan pillar at Vaishali, Bihar, Wikimedia Commons

Page 13, National Flag of India, Wikimedia Commons

Page 14, Emblem of India, Wikimedia Commons

Page 17, Indian soldiers at a shore post in Berbera, August 1940, Wikimedia Commons

Page 18, Gandhi leading the 1930 Salt March, Wikimedia Commons

Page 20, The Lion capital at Sarnath, Wikimedia Commons

Page 21, Ashokan Lions at Sarnath, Wikimedia Commons

Page 23, Replica of Dharma Chakra at Duvvada hillock in Visakhapatnam, Wikimedia Commons

Page 31, Mundaka Upanisad, Atharvaveda, Wikimedia Commons

Page 37, The Asokan Pillar at Feroz Shah Kotla, Wikimedia Commons

Page 43, The Coat of Arms of the United Kingdom by Sawrey Gilpin, Wikimedia Commons

Page 47, The Preamble of the Constitution of India, Wikimedia Commons

Page 49, Images from page 113 from the Constitution of India, Wikimedia Commons

Page 51, The National Emblem illustrated by Dinanath Bhargava, Wikimedia Commons

Page 53, 'Gandhiji Praying' by Nandalal Bose, Wikimedia Commons

Page 55, 1000 India Rupee Currency Note, Wikimedia Commons

Page 55, 2 Indian Rupee Coin, Wikimedia Commons

Page 55, Stamp of India, 2017, Wikimedia Commons

Page 55, Indian Passport, Wikimedia Commons

Page 55, 10 Indian Paise Coin, Wikimedia Commons

Page 57, The Indian Emblem on the Vidhan Soudha, Bengaluru, PxHere

Page 57, The Vidhan Soudha, Bengaluru, Wikimedia Commons

ALSO READ IN THE SERIES

The Story of India's National Flag

by Kavitha Mandana

Who created India's National Flag?
What does the flag signify?
What are the stories that lie behind the making of the Indian tricolour?

In this beautifully illustrated book filled with little known facts from Indian history, pictures and photographs, read some unusual stories: The first flag that was created in 1906 by a pair of nationalists—Hemchandra Kanungo and Sachindra Prasad Bose. About Sister Nivedita, the Irish teacher who became a disciple of Swami Vivekananda and created a flag for the freedom movement. Kartar Singh, the nineteen year old revolutionary who joined the Ghadar Party that also made a flag for a free India. And about the genius of flag designer Pingali Venkayya, who was a linguist, geologist and agriscientist as well, and who made 30 different Indian flag designs.

Read about the days leading up to India's Independence in 1947, when the Flag Committee of the Constituent Assembly worked quickly to create a new flag for a free India. Their final design was a flag that would proclaim the country's underlying values of peace, non-violence and sacrifice through the graceful tricolour.